When good people have
a falling out, only *one* of them
may be at fault at first; but
if the strife continues long,
usually *BOTH* become guilty.

~ Thomas Fuller

WALKTHETALK.COM

Resources for Personal and Professional Success

What To Do When CONFLICT HAPPENS

Inquiries regarding permission for use of the material contained in this book should be addressed to:

The WALK THE TALK Company
1100 Parker Square, Suite 250
Flower Mound, Texas 75028
972.899.8300

WALK THE TALK books may be purchased for educational, business, or sales promotion use.

WALK THE TALK®, The WALK THE TALK Company® and WalkTheTalk.com™ are trademarks of
Performance Systems Corporation.

Printed in the United States of America
10 9 8 7 6 5 4 3

ISBN 1-885228-77-5

90000

9 781885 228772

Edited by Michelle Sedas
Cover design by Stephen Wulf
Printed by MultiAd

WHAT TO DO WHEN

CONFLICT

HAPPENS

EVERY EMPLOYEE'S GUIDE TO
RESOLVING WORKPLACE PROBLEMS

Framing the Facts

Introduction

Maybe it has already happened. Maybe it's waiting down the road where you work. Whenever it occurs, your focus will be interrupted, your stomach will churn, and your ability to do your very best work will be hampered. It will stick in your mind – affecting both your attitude and your behavior.

The "it" is interpersonal **conflict** ... a business reality that has been around for as long as organizations have existed. And it's one of the most important – yet poorly handled – problems facing workplaces (and work*ers*) today.

Wherever there are people, there *will* be conflict. Count on it. Expect it. After all, each of us sees the world through a somewhat different pair of glasses. We all have special needs, diverse goals, individual values, and varying perceptions of what's right, fair, and appropriate. And occasionally, those needs, goals, values, and perceptions are going to clash. It's inevitable for our personal lives ... it's inevitable for our jobs.

Sooner or later, you will find yourself involved in a conflict (a.k.a. having a "beef") with someone at work. Maybe the person will offend or otherwise "wrong" you in some way. Perhaps you'll feel that he or she has inappropriately interfered with your plans and activities. Or it could be that a difference of opinion about a workplace issue will grow into a strong and emotionally charged disagreement. Regardless of the nature of the conflict, or what led up to it, there *will* be a problem – and it *will* need to be addressed. The logical question:

What are you going to do?

Any time you find yourself at odds with someone at work, there are several response choices available to you:

You can avoid the issue – hoping that the problem will just go away on its own.

You can adopt a "poor me" victim's mentality – lamenting your plight to anyone who will listen (except, of course, the person you have the problem with).

You can explode – allowing heated emotions to dictate your attitude and actions.

Or, you can get even – finding ways to disturb the person who has disturbed you.

Clearly, none of those all-too-common responses is effective or desirable – especially if your goals are to end the conflict, eliminate the negative impact the problem is producing, AND maintain a decent relationship with the other person. But, here's the good news: you have another option … another choice! You *can* calmly, respectfully, and constructively confront the other person – and work with him or her to resolve the issue. **This book will show you how to do just that**!

Through the information presented on the pages that follow, you will:

■ Gain a greater understanding of what conflict is – and how it affects your organization, your coworkers, and YOU.

■ Clarify your responsibilities when it comes to conflict-laden situations.

■ Learn proven strategies and techniques for solving problems, improving cooperation, and creating win-win outcomes.

Pay attention to what you're about to read. It will serve you well. The nights of lost sleep over issues with colleagues are about to end.

The journey to more effective, productive, and satisfying working relationships begins now!

Contents

Facing
the Fallacies

10 Common Misconceptions
About Conflict in the Workplace

Misconception 1:

"Conflict is *inherently* bad and unhealthy."

There are those who feel that conflict of any kind is both disruptive and destructive. But, as the old song title goes, *It ain't necessarily so!*

The fact is, conflict can be both beneficial and desirable. Whether it comes in the form of differing viewpoints, honest disagreements, complaints, disputes, or internal "cognitive dissonance" – conflict challenges the status quo; it forces us to examine our thinking and behavior ... to reflect on *what* we do and *how* we do it. And more times than not, it's conflict that is the genesis of innovation and positive change. So, is conflict inherently bad (the key word being *inherently*)? Absolutely not! Are there times, however, when conflict *is* unhealthy and destructive? Of course!

With few exceptions, the most counterproductive forms of conflict found in organizations typically involve "beefs" between coworkers. The scenario is all too common: someone says or does something that ticks someone else off. As a result, communication and cooperation between the parties dwindle and, eventually, the quality and quantity of their work is negatively impacted. That's why it's imperative that *interpersonal* issues be addressed and lasting resolution achieved – which is what the majority of this book is all about.

And so, when it comes to "conflict," the challenges for all of us are clear: 1) welcome, accept, and utilize its positive aspects to enhance our results, and 2) minimize and/or eliminate those negative aspects which far too often are obstacles to our success.

"Conflict doesn't occur that often in the workplace."

In the real world, nothing could be further from the truth! Wherever there are people who must interact with one another, day in and day out, there *will* be conflict. That's just simply a fact of life.

When you think about it, business organizations (and the teams that comprise them) are collections of individuals from diverse backgrounds who bring unique ideas, needs, expectations, and individual personalities with them to the job. For every assertive person, there's another employee who's more passive; for every risk taker, there's someone else who prefers a more conservative approach; for every immediate reactor, there's an in-depth analyzer; for every ... oh well, you get the picture.

When all of these different human traits and behaviors come together, there will, unquestionably, be clashes. It's inevitable that a bunch of people are going to step on a bunch of *other* people's toes – a bunch of times. That's perfectly natural and no real problem in and of itself. What *is* cause for concern, however, is the fact that so many of those naturally occurring conflicts are not effectively resolved and, instead, are allowed to fester.

People who feel that negative conflicts don't occur that often in the workplace are either oblivious to the existence of issues, or they just choose to ignore them. Either way, that's a huge problem.

Focus 90% of your time on solutions and
only 10% of your time on problems.

~ Anthony J. D'Angelo

 **Solution FINDER**

FREE...List of 15 Common "Out of Sync" Personal and Professional Behaviors
Go to www.walkthetalk.com

Misconception 3:

"Conflict is always a matter of *right vs. wrong*."

When you think about interpersonal conflict between two people, what comes to mind? What can you conclude from your own experiences of friction with a coworker? Do you presume that there's always an "instigator" who is in the wrong and a "victim" who has done *nothing* wrong – and therefore is right? Do you blame the "instigator" for the conflict and believe that he or she, alone, bears the responsibility for making a behavior change? If you answered yes to either (or both) of those last two questions, you might want to do some rethinking.

While it's true that *some* conflicts are clearly issues of right vs. wrong, it's not always the case. And assuming otherwise is a dangerous and counterproductive mindset to have. Why? Because, often, "right" and "wrong" are *relative* terms; they're perceptual issues. And with few exceptions, people tend to believe that they are right most of the time. It's usually "the other guy" who's at fault. After all, "I've done nothing wrong, so there's nothing I need to do about this. It's all him … it's all her!"

The problem is that "him" or "her" is thinking the exact same thing! As a result, neither party makes an effort to address and resolve their differences. And in the end, BOTH parties end up being at fault.

So, clearly, conflicts are not always a matter of right vs. wrong. Many times, they are about two competing wrongs … or even two competing rights. Either way, **it takes two to tangle!**

 Solution FINDER

"Conflicts are the result of clashing personalities."

False! In fact, just the opposite is true: interpersonal conflicts *aren't* the result of personality clashes at all. "Whoa!" you say. "That bold statement can't possibly be correct!" Well, don't close the book – obviously, an explanation is in order.

Think about it for a moment. Just what is a *personality*, anyway? Can you touch one? Can you hold it? Can you take a picture of it? Can you do a persectomy and cut one out? Of course not! That's because "personality" is a nebulous, intangible concept. It's a judgment ... a conclusion ... a label – that stems from a series of specific, observable **behaviors**. It's what a person *does* that leads to generalizations about his or her personality, and it's what people actually *do* (or *don't* do) that is at the core of conflict.

Bottom line: Conflicts are the result of behaviors – not personality clashes. And that's a good news story. Why? Because when it comes to resolving problems, it's a lot easier for people to change their daily actions and behaviors than it is to overhaul their individual "personalities."

To the best of my knowledge, nobody
ever 'personalitied' his or her way into
trouble ... or out of it!

~ Paul Sims

"Conflict is most prevalent in crisis situations."

Just about everyone (and every group), at one time or another, faces some type of "crisis" situation at work. Typically, when things turn bad, our backs are against the proverbial wall. Issues, demands, and challenges are coming at us at a fast and furious pace. Often, there's little time for analysis, consensus building, ensuring political correctness, or just plain being "nice" when we're putting out fires. We must move quickly as we act, react, adjust, and respond to whatever comes our way. Put all that together and it's safe to conclude that crises offer the highest and most common potential for interpersonal conflict ... right? Not really!

Think about the last workplace "crisis" you were involved with. If you're like most folks, you'll recall that everyone in your group tended to pull together – to assume whatever role that was needed ... to do whatever was necessary to make it through. Chances are you let more things slide, cut each other more "slack," and were a lot less sensitive to coworker behaviors that you would, at other times, consider to be disturbing. Why? Because your backs were against the wall, *together* – and because you all had a unified purpose ... a common goal: survival. Once the crisis subsided, however, people probably began reverting back to their normal behaviors, their old habits, and their heightened sensitivities. That's perfectly normal. And that's why a "perfectly normal" (*non*-crisis) situation is where you're most likely to find conflict rearing its ugly head.

So, if you're looking to minimize conflict where you work, pay special attention to what's happening when things are running *smoothly*.

"Most conflicts resolve *themselves* over time."

Yeah, right ... if only that were true! Don't you just wish that all inter-personal problems were self-repairing? Things would be so much easier. We probably wouldn't lose as much sleep, or have as many knots in our stomachs, or have as many days when we go home feeling beat up and emotionally drained. There would be less tension ... less stress. We wouldn't need the courage to confront issues. We wouldn't need the skills and strategies necessary to solve problems. And one more thing: We wouldn't be in the real world!

Here's one you can take to the bank: Unlike fine wine, conflicts that are left alone rarely improve with age. They're much more likely to fester and decay. Sure, we can ignore them – or learn to live with them – but the odds are miniscule that they'll evaporate into thin air and then all will be well with the world again.

Fact is, conflicts must be resolved the same way they were started in the first place – through human actions. They must be confronted, addressed, and worked through. Will doing so be pleasant? Probably not. Is that a good enough reason for avoiding issues? *Absolutely* not!

Remember this: When it comes to conflict, time heals all wounds – as long as they are *treated* first.

Problems do not go away. They must be worked through or else they remain, forever a barrier to the growth and development of the spirit.

~ M. Scott Peck

Misconception 7:

"People usually know when they've disturbed someone else."

The key word that makes this statement a fallacy is "usually." Certainly, there are times when it's clear that we've disturbed a colleague and set the wheels of conflict in motion. We see or hear the other person's reaction to something we've done – or perhaps we're clued in by another coworker – and we realize there's a problem brewing. But there are also many times when we have absolutely no idea that we've hurt, offended, or otherwise disturbed someone else. Nothing is said, no reactions are seen, and we continue to go along our merry way – only later to be surprised with the news that bad feelings have been churning.

You see, we all tend to judge ourselves by our intentions. If our intentions are good and noble (which they usually are), then in our minds, the actions resulting from those intentions must also be good and noble. But others have no way of knowing what our true intentions are, so they judge us by their perceptions of, and reactions to, what we do. Sometimes those perceptions are negative. And if the "offendee" fails to say something, we're left totally in the dark.

So, what's the key learning here? It's simply this: Don't assume that people always know when they've done things to sow the seeds of conflict. If you have a problem with someone, it's up to YOU to tactfully surface the issue. Otherwise, you'll end up doing nothing to help resolve the conflict – waiting, instead, for him or her to make the first move. And if that other person is clueless to your feelings, you'll be waiting for a very long time.

Misconception 8:

"Conflicts only impact the disputing parties."

If that statement were true, there would be much less concern about conflict – and much less emphasis on conflict resolution – in many organizations today. You probably wouldn't have been given this book. Heck, we might not have even written it! After all, if two people have a beef with each other and they don't see eye to eye, what's the big deal? Well, the *big deal* is this: Unresolved conflicts affect many more people than just the "combatants." A lot of folks are negatively impacted when coworkers are at odds with one another.

Certainly, it all starts with the **disputing parties** themselves. Conflict hampers communication and cooperation; it hinders each person's ability to do his or her best, most creative work – and to experience the full satisfaction that normally comes with it. But the problem doesn't stop there. The tension and stress of conflict spills over onto **other members of the team** as well. They *know* what's going on, they don't want to "take sides" or "walk on eggshells," and they must deal with – and often compensate for – the counterproductive behaviors that typically result from other people's conflict. And that makes it difficult for them to do *their* best work, too.

And then, of course, there are **internal and external customers** – those who are the unfortunate recipients of the goods and services provided by a struggling, out-of-sync team. Your customers may never know that a conflict is taking place within your work group, but they probably *would* care if they knew. Why? Because like many other people, they are affected!

Misconception 9:

"Resolving employee conflict is management's responsibility."

In response to that statement, we offer this timeless lesson from *Reality 101*: As adults, each of us is responsible for our own lives and careers. We "own" the choices we make, the actions we take, and – for the most part – the situations we find ourselves in. So, whenever our behaviors prove to be problematic or our situations become less than desirable, each of us, individually, is also responsible for doing something about it … for fixing what's broken.

As members of an organization, employees are expected to maintain positive and productive working relationships with their coworkers. Doing so is critical to overall business success. It's a basic requirement of the job – one that *isn't* being met whenever conflict is present. So, when two or more employees have a problem with each other, it's up to THEM to talk about it and work through it. Sometimes that actually happens. Many times, it doesn't.

It's no secret that dealing with conflict is an unpleasant task. As a result, many people avoid it any way they can. One of the most common rationales (i.e., "excuses") offered for such inaction is this: *That's what my boss gets paid for. Solving problems is management's responsibility, not mine.* Well, that's just not the case when it comes to interpersonal issues between adults. Sure, managers *do* have a role to play. They need to encourage cooperation and open communication. They need to show people how to solve problems. And they need to intervene when team members are either unable or unwilling to resolve their differences. But none of that changes the fact that the primary responsibility for conflict resolution *always* rests with those directly involved in the issues.

Misconception 10:

"Conflicts continue mostly because of stubbornness and a lack of caring."

Is stubbornness a reason why some conflicts occur and then continue without being properly addressed? Yes. Will there be times when one (or more) of the people involved in a conflict doesn't care enough to do anything about the problem? Occasionally. Are stubbornness and a lack of caring the *main* reasons that so many conflicts remain unresolved? NO!

Most of us really *do* care about the relationships we have with our colleagues. After all, we spend a large portion of our waking hours interacting with, and relying upon, our fellow teammates. We want those hours to be as pleasant and trouble-free as possible. When they're not, we're bothered ... we feel it. And the feeling isn't good. In fact, it's lousy!

But, if conflict makes us so uncomfortable, why is it we don't always address and resolve problems as soon as they surface? The answer is this: **We lack the skills and confidence needed to effectively address the issues we face**. We're not sure WHAT it is we should do ... we don't know HOW to achieve the resolution we want. The thought of confronting others often causes more discomfort than the problem itself. And so we do nothing – sometimes allowing a veil of stubbornness to hide the real, underlying issue: we're just plain scared.

Are you confident in your ability to handle any future workplace conflicts in which you may become involved? If your answer is "yes," congratulations! The pages that follow should reinforce what you already know. If your answer is "no," we have more good news: you're about to learn what to do!

It takes TWO
to quarrel,
but only ONE
to end it.

~ Spanish Proverb

Finding the Fix

The C.A.L.M. Model

The C.A.L.M. Model

Okay, now we know that conflicts are natural, they occur frequently, they affect a lot of people, they don't resolve themselves, and the parties involved bear the primary responsibility for working things out. We also know that conflicts are, by their very nature, emotionally charged occurrences that must be dealt with deliberately and carefully. Handle them the *right* way and everyone wins. Handle them the *wrong* way and things can actually get worse. All of that, of course, leads to *the* question: What does it take to handle conflict "the right way"? The answer: It takes proven strategies ... it takes guidelines ... it takes **a plan**.

Probably the worst thing anyone can do in a conflict situation is act (or react) without thinking. "Knee-jerk" responses rarely serve us well – especially when human feelings and emotions are involved. The chances are just too high that we'll end up saying or doing something that we'll later regret. So, whenever someone does something that bothers you, you find yourself in a heated disagreement, or you merely sense a level of tension developing between you and a coworker, some thinking, analysis, and action planning are in order. To help you do that, we offer the following four-step **C.A.L.M. Model**:

CLARIFY the Issue

ADDRESS the Problem

LISTEN to the Other Side

MANAGE Your Way to Resolution

CLARIFY the Issue

The keys to any problem-solving process are *defining* and *understanding* (clarifying) the issue you're dealing with. And that's especially true when it comes to interpersonal conflicts. The better you understand a problem, the greater your chances of choosing an appropriate course of action to correct it. It's just that simple.

Your first encounter with conflict will usually be on an emotional level. You'll *feel* it. It will bother you. You'll want it to go away. And you may be tempted to react to the situation the same way you're experiencing it: emotionally. But rarely will that approach lead to the resolution you want. Perhaps Albert Einstein put it best when he said:

> *Problems cannot be solved at the same level of consciousness that created them.*

Dissecting the Conflict

Before you charge off and begin reacting, you need to step back and **think** – you need to calmly and rationally examine what's happening, why it's happening, why you feel the way you do, and what you need to keep in mind as you address the issue.

In other words, you need to move the conflict from your heart (i.e., your emotions) to your head. And the way you do *that* is by going somewhere private and quiet, grabbing a pad and pencil (or a keyboard and screen), and answering – in writing – the questions you'll find on the next two pages.

CONFLICT CLARIFICATION QUESTIONS

Primary Questions:

➤ What am I upset about? In specific, behavioral terms, what actually happened? Who else is involved? What did they do?

➤ What exactly am I feeling (anger, frustration, fear, etc.)? Why am I feeling that way?

➤ How might I have contributed to the problem?

➤ Is there a chance that I'm overreacting to the situation? If so, why might that be the case?

➤ In terms of actions and relationships, what are my desired outcomes for this situation? What will successful resolution look and feel like?

➤ If I were the other person involved in the conflict, how would I want to be approached and dealt with?

Secondary Questions:

➤ Where might the other person have been "coming from"? Might he or she have been motivated by good intentions?

➤ Has this happened before or is it a first-time occurrence?

➤ How is the situation affecting me and my work? Are others impacted? If so, how?

➤ When dealing with this issue, what might I do to increase the chances that I'll get the results I want? What counter-productive behaviors do I want to be sure to avoid?

> Additional questions I feel are relevant:

Once you've answered these questions – along with any additional ones you may have developed yourself – go back and review your responses. Reflect on what you wrote. Doing that will give you a better "handle" on the problem you're facing. It will help you address the situation rationally instead of emotionally. And you'll be better prepared to discuss the issue with the other people involved.

Molehills and Mountains

Occasionally, after people calm down and analyze what has taken place, they find that issues don't seem nearly as bad or disturbing as they had originally thought. As they work their way through the "Conflict Clarification Questions," they discover that the impact on them (and others) is pretty much nonexistent, or that the other person probably *was* motivated by good intentions, or that the problem was a one-time occurrence that likely won't be repeated ... or all of the above.

If that ever happens to you – if you find that the more you think about an issue, the more it appears to be a NON-issue – your best bet is to merely chalk the whole thing up to a probable overreaction on your part. And your best response is to do *nothing* – other than to cut the other person a little slack.

A word of caution here: Be sure that fear of confrontation isn't the basis of your "no problem" assessment and resulting decision to let things slide. Not every conflict will be small and insignificant. There are more than enough "mountains" out there – real issues that must be dealt with. And fooling yourself into believing that *a mountain is just a molehill* merely so you can feel better about looking the other way and doing nothing will eventually come back to haunt you.

So, remember: If you're facing a legitimate NON-issue, don't worry about it! Let it be – unless and until it happens again.

But, if you have a *real* issue that's affecting you and perhaps others on the team, move to the next three steps in the **C.A.L.M. Model**. Ask the other person involved in the conflict if you can have a short meeting to discuss an issue you're facing, and then ...

ADDRESS the Problem

Without question, the most critical activity of any conflict-resolution process is the **discussion**. Avoid any temptations to handle the matter through one-way communication such as e-mail, notes, or messages left on voice mail. You need to talk directly *with* the other person in order to share your concerns and get things worked out.

The initial portion of the discussion is where you address the problem. And that entails two components: 1) the opening, and 2) a description of the issue that's troubling you.

1. THE OPENING

The first few seconds of the conversation are critical to your ultimate success. Avoid starting with finger pointing "you statements" such as: *You did something that really bothers me,* or, *There's something you did that we need to talk about.* While those words may be true, they also tend to make people tense and defensive. Instead, use a non-accusatory opening that asks for the other person's cooperation:

I need your help to solve a problem I'm facing.

2. THE ISSUE DESCRIPTION

Once you've opened the conversation (and the other person has responded in some way), immediately describe in specific, factual, and non-accusatory terms:

- Exactly what happened.
- How what happened made you feel.
- How it has negatively affected you and your work, and others and their work.

10 Things to Remember (and DO) When Conducting Conflict-Resolution Discussions

1. **Make sure the environment is right.**

   Pick a time that's convenient (for both of you) – and, whenever possible, a place that's free of distractions and the potential for interruptions.

2. **Have a walk-in strategy.**

   Plan what you'll say and do BEFORE you meet. Think of the exact words you'll use to open the conversation – and practice saying them. And formulate contingency responses to various ways the other person may act and react.

3. **Get to the point.**

   Don't allow the issue to become clouded with excessive small talk. You can be respectful, polite, and tactful – and still be DIRECT.

4. **Attack the problem, not the person.**

   Stay focused on what actually occurred. Avoid accusations or assigning blame. Minimize the use of the word "you" when starting the discussion. And when describing the problem, use "you" only to describe what the person actually did.

5. **Share your feelings … and how you're impacted.**

   Use "I" statements to describe how what happened has made you feel and how it has affected you. Example: *When that happened, I really felt belittled, embarrassed, and underappreciated.*

6. **Stay away from hearsay.**

   Don't make or strengthen your case by discussing what coworkers may have said to you about the matter. Certainly you can mention how others are specifically impacted. But be sure to avoid expressing their opinions for them.

7. **Pay attention to your body language.**

   Avoid negative "message-sending gestures" such as arm crossing, finger tapping, head shaking, and eye rolling.

8. **Control your emotions.**

   Certainly that's easier said than done – especially when you're caught off guard. So, expect the unexpected. Assume – going into the discussion – that something may happen to trigger your emotions, and have a plan for exactly what you'll do to avoid "losing it."

9. **Keep the desired end-state in mind.**

   Throughout the discussion, periodically remind yourself that your goal is to get an issue resolved in a respectful, collaborative manner – not to "win" an argument or debate. Make sure that everything you do, say, and agree to is in sync with that goal.

10. **Think "dialogue" – not "monologue."**

   Remember that effective communication is a two-way street. The other person may also have feelings and concerns about the matter – ones that will need to be discussed before resolution is achieved. So, be sure to concentrate as much on *hearing* as you do on making sure you're heard.

LISTEN to the Other Side

In all likelihood, the other person will respond to your opening statement and description of the issue in one of two ways:

1. He or she will quickly apologize for unknowingly disturbing you.

If that happens, the conflict is resolved (at least for now). There's no need to continue with the process. Just accept the apology, extend your hand, and say something like: *Thank you, Michael. I value you as a colleague, and I really appreciate your cooperation.*

2. He or she will have concerns that need to be surfaced and discussed.

Perhaps the person feels that you're overreacting, or that there's a good reason for his or her actions, or that YOU did something that precipitated the conflict. He or she may volunteer this information – or sensing there's an unexpressed concern, you may need to probe for it by saying, *I'd really like to hear your thoughts and feelings about this.* Either way, it's important that you make a sincere effort to hear and understand whatever it is the person has to say ... it's imperative that you LISTEN!

When You ARE "The Other Person"

Listening is equally important for *both* parties involved in any conflict-resolution discussion. And there may be times when, instead of being the one who initiates the discussion, you *are* "the other person" – you're approached by someone else who has a problem with something *you've* done. If that happens, make a sincere effort to hear and understand his or her concerns. You'll help increase the chances that everyone will benefit, and you'll earn the right to expect reciprocation sometime down the road.

Listening Tips

True listening is an active process that requires focus and concentration. It's important that you concentrate on the words and behaviors of the speaker in order to understand where he or she is coming from and why this person feels as he or she does. And once you have that knowledge, you'll be better able to resolve differences and work together more productively.

Here are a few tips to help you listen effectively:

- **Give Your Total Attention.** Establish and maintain eye contact with the speaker. Concentrate on the words he or she is saying ... and the overall message. Pretend that you'll be tested on everything the person says.

- **NEVER Interrupt!** Interrupting – including finishing a person's sentences – is disrespectful, frustrating, and counterproductive to effective communication.

- **Ask Questions for Clarification.** If the person says something you don't understand, seek clarification in a non-challenging way: *Scott, I'm not sure I really understand. Could you go over that again?*

- **Paraphrase.** Repeat, in your own words, what someone says – to this person's satisfaction. *Kate, let me make sure I understand. You're saying that .... Is that correct?*

- ***Show* That You're Listening.** Lean forward, nod your head, and respond to what is said with an occasional "Okay," "I see," "Uh huh," "I understand," etc.

MANAGE Your Way to Resolution

Certain conflicts are easier to resolve than others. If the problem involves an unconscious, disturbing behavior exhibited by a coworker, there's a good chance that – after you talk things through – the other person will offer an apology ... and a commitment to avoid repeating the offending action in the future. BINGO! Case closed.

Sometimes, however, conflicts stem from honest and strong differences of opinion about work-related issues. And those typically require more effort, more discussion, and more cooperation (by both parties) before resolution can be achieved.

Imagine for a moment that a coworker approaches you with an issue. He or she has a problem with something you did or didn't do. After listening carefully, you conclude that your actions were right, appropriate, and justified. Are you merely going to apologize and commit to changing your behavior? Probably not! And neither will the other person whenever roles are reversed and *you're* the one raising the concern.

Differences of opinion typically exist on a "level playing field." Both parties *feel* they are right. Both will likely be impacted if the problem continues. And, whenever possible, both must be satisfied with the outcome. For that to happen, you must do more than just share your concerns, listen, and then wait for a response. You'll also need to orchestrate a mutually beneficial outcome ... you'll need to manage your way to resolution by:

1. **Gaining agreement that a problem exists.**
2. **Identifying each other's concerns and needs.**
3. **Exploring possible win-win solutions.**
4. **Agreeing on a course of action.**
5. **Determining how missteps will be handled.**
6. **Closing on a positive note.**

Gaining agreement that a problem exists

Before the other person will be willing to work with you to identify and agree upon a solution, he or she must believe that a solution is *needed*; he or she must concur that a problem exists – and that it should be addressed. To gain that concurrence, say something like:

> *I'm feeling some real tension between the two of us.*
> *Do you agree that we have issues – and that it's in both*
> *of our best interests to work things out?*

> *Note: Rarely will the other person say "no." But should that occur, redescribe the problem (what happened) and its impact, and then ask for the person's help. If he or she still won't acknowledge the problem or agree to work with you, end the discussion and seek counsel and assistance from your supervisor.*

Identifying each other's concerns and needs

In order to develop a solution that meets both parties' needs, you have to know what those needs are. Identify the criteria of a mutually beneficial solution by asking the following questions, listening to the person's responses, and then sharing *your* answers with him or her:

> *When it comes to working through this issue, what's most important for you? What concerns do you have that must be satisfied? What needs must be met? What does a win-win solution look like to you?*

Exploring possible win-win solutions

Now that you know what's important to each other, you can begin to identify possible solutions:

> *What are some specific things we might do individually –*
> *and together – to get past this, and to help each other*
> *be more successful in the future?*

Agreeing on a course of action

Once you identify a solution that seems to work for both of you (and involves action on both of your parts), "lock" the agreement:

> *I'm really confident that this will work well for us.*
> *You can count on me to keep my end of the bargain.*
> *Can I count on you to do the same?*

> *Note: If you are unable to identify a workable solution at your initial meeting, schedule a second meeting to continue the process. If a second meeting produces no results, suggest that you both meet with your supervisor (or another neutral "third party") who can serve as a mediator.*

Determining how missteps will be handled

Agree, up front, what you will do if either party fails to live up to his or her agreement:

> *Because we're human, there's always a possibility that, down the road, one or both of us might slip up. What should we do ... how should we handle it if either of us unconsciously violates the commitment we made today?*

Closing on a positive note

Summarize the agreements made, and then end the discussion in a way that will encourage both of you to leave feeling good about what took place. Extend your hand and say something like:

> *Maria, I really appreciate your time – and your willingness to work with me on this. A lot was accomplished ... and we did it together. I hope you feel as good about today as I do. Thank you.*

PUT IT IN WRITING

Consider documenting the behavioral changes/actions that you both agree to – and give a copy to the other person. That way, you'll confirm that a real, tangible outcome has resulted from your meeting. And should the problem reoccur, you'll have a written record you can refer to in subsequent discussions with the person ... or with others who may need to intervene.

THE C.A.L.M. MODEL

CLARIFY THE ISSUE
- Think – minimize emotions by dissecting the problem
- Answer the "Conflict Clarification Questions" (in writing)
- Ignore NON-issues (overreactions on your part)

ADDRESS THE PROBLEM
- Meet with the other person
- Use a non-accusatory opening
- Describe what happened, its impact, and how you feel

LISTEN TO THE OTHER SIDE
- Be open to the other person's concerns
- Employ effective listening techniques
- Be sure to listen if you are "the other person"

MANAGE YOUR WAY TO RESOLUTION
- Gain agreement that a problem exists
- Identify each other's concerns and needs
- Explore possible win-win solutions
- Agree on a course of action
- Determine how missteps will be handled
- Close on a positive note

When There's No Time to Plan

Occasionally, people are caught off guard – finding themselves smack dab in the middle of an unexpected conflict. Sound familiar? You're in it before you know it, and there's no time for formulating a well-thought-out resolution strategy (i.e., the C.A.L.M. Model). You've got to respond in some way, and you have to do it NOW! What do you do? How can you keep the situation from escalating? Here are a few suggestions that should help:

1. **Stop, breathe, and think.** Stop whatever it is you're doing, take a couple of deep breaths to control your tension, and then immediately think about exactly what you need to do and say next.

2. **Acknowledge the conflict** by saying something like: *Michael, I'm sensing that there are some issues between the two of us that we need to talk through,* or, *Kate, I'm feeling that I might have done something to upset you. Can we talk about it?*

3. **Buy some time.** Suggest that you meet at a later time that day (or the following day) so that you both have an opportunity to relax a little and gather your thoughts. If the other person agrees, use the time to prepare for the meeting by working through the C.A.L.M. Model. If the person doesn't agree on a time delay …

4. **Take it somewhere else** (if other coworkers are present). That way, you'll avoid disrupting the rest of the group – and you'll eliminate any urges you and the other person might have to "showboat" or maintain some bogus image in front of your teammates. Suggest a different venue with words such as: *It's best for everyone if we keep this just between us. Where else would you feel comfortable talking?*

5. **Keep it respectful.** Do your absolute best to conduct yourself in a calm and respectful manner – regardless of how the other person responds. Will it be easy? Of course not! But that doesn't change the fact that although you can't control what others do, you certainly can (and do) control your own behavior.

Forging the Future

What Leaders Can Do to Minimize Conflict in Their Work Groups

Certainly, when it comes to interpersonal conflicts, employees have the primary responsibility for resolving issues that develop with coworkers. But leaders play an important role as well.

First and foremost, every leader must encourage cooperation and open communication within his or her work group. Doing so will help to reduce the number of conflicts that otherwise might occur and increase the overall effectiveness of the team. If you're a leader you may be thinking: "That's great. But how do I do it?" Here are a few ideas that should help:

- **Clarify your expectations.** Make sure each team member knows that cooperation and communication are job requirements.

- **Set the example.** Model the behaviors you expect from others.

- **Reinforce desired performance.** Recognize and reward team members who work well with others.

- **Hold everyone accountable.** Include "teamwork," "cooperation," and "open communication" as feedback categories on all performance reviews you conduct. And make sure there are consequences for failing to meet expectations.

The "M Strategies"

Sometimes, despite your best leadership efforts to encourage a cooperative work environment, you'll find that you must become directly involved in the conflict-resolution process. Depending on the circumstances – including any "conflict warning signs" (next page) you detect – you may need to engage in one or more of the following three **M Strategies**:

MENTORING (coaching) **for Conflict Resolution**
Teaching employees how to resolve conflicts themselves

MEDIATING for Conflict Resolution
Intervening to help employees resolve their differences

MANDATING Cooperation
Forcing uncooperative employees to respond appropriately

Watching for the Warning Signs

Because the potential for negative conflict exists within any work group, leaders must keep an eye out for indicators that intervention may be warranted on their part. Here are a few "conflict warning signs" that should trigger an investigation to determine if there is a need for you to get involved:

- ☒ You're told (or you overhear a conversation) about a problem existing between two or more members of your work group.

- ☒ Work requiring cooperation between employees is behind schedule, incomplete, or poorly done.

- ☒ At staff meetings, team members are uncharacteristically quiet, openly criticize a coworker's actions and ideas, or purposely sit far away from each other.

- ☒ Someone displays negative body language (e.g., eye rolling, head shaking, arm crossing) when a coworker is speaking.

- ☒ Team members avoid, ignore, or obviously exclude one another during breaks and lunches.

- ☒ Someone on the team has clearly been left out of "the information loop."

- ☒ Activities are scheduled and performed at a time when a team member is known to be unavailable.

And the most obvious of all …

- ☒ You get a note, e-mail, or verbal request suggesting that: "You need to do something about (<u>employee name</u>)!"

FREE...7 Ways to Minimize the Need for Performance Improvement Sessions
Go to www.walkthetalk.com

MENTORING (coaching) **for Conflict Resolution**

When to do it:

- No conflict exists, but you want to prepare individual team members to handle issues that may arise down the road (proactive strategy).

- You learn that a minor conflict is developing between coworkers – and that neither party has done anything to address it.

- Someone comes to you with a problem with a coworker. You ask if he or she has talked to the other person. The answer: *NO … I'm not sure what to do,* or, *I'm not comfortable handling it.*

A Few Tips on How to do it:

➤ Meet with everyone individually. (Ask each person to read/reread this book before your session.) Emphasize the importance of coworkers resolving their own issues and state your confidence that, with preparation, anyone can do it. Discuss any fears the person may have about confronting coworkers. Indicate that the best way to overcome that fear is to work through it.

➤ Have the person briefly describe the issue he or she is facing. Note: If you are conducting a proactive developmental (training) session, ask the person to create a fictional scenario to work on – perhaps a conflict he or she has experienced in the past.

➤ Guide the person through all of the **C.A.L.M. Model** components. Have him or her answer the "Conflict Clarification Questions." Review the discussion and listening techniques, and then role-play the conversation – with you playing the part of "the other person." Then, critique the practice discussion – identifying things that can be done even better in the actual discussion.

➤ Ask for the person's commitment to address the issue with the other involved party within a specified timeframe. Set a follow-up meeting to find out how things went.

MEDIATING for Conflict Resolution

When to do it:

- One of your employees has a problem with a coworker, and – despite your best coaching efforts – is too scared or uncomfortable to confront the issue on his or her own.

- Two employees are engaged in an ongoing conflict, it's affecting their work (and perhaps the work of others), and they have been unable to resolve their differences by themselves.

A Few Tips on How to do it:

➤ Schedule a meeting with both parties (together). Explain the purpose and instruct each person to complete the "Conflict Clarification Questions" in writing prior to the session. Then, bring both parties together. Describe the problem (and its negative impact) as you see it. Clarify your expectation that both employees will cooperate with each other to resolve their differences and work together effectively in the future.

➤ Ask each person to share his or her perspectives on, and feelings about, the problem. Instruct the parties that: 1) they must look at and talk with each other instead of you, and 2) each person must listen to and repeat back what the other says before he or she can respond.

➤ After the problem has been discussed, ask each person to describe what he or she can do to help bring resolution to the issue. If the parties' responses are satisfactory to each other, ask for their commitments to follow through. If one or both responses are *not* satisfactory, continue probing and pursuing alternatives – using the C.A.L.M. Model techniques – until both parties arrive at an agreeable course of action.

➤ Close the meeting by asking the parties to shake hands, thanking them for their cooperation, and setting a follow-up date for everyone to get together and discuss how things are progressing. Then, make a written record of the discussion – in case future reference is needed.

MANDATING Cooperation

When to do it:

- Two employees are engaged in an ongoing conflict, it's negatively affecting your operation, and one (or both) of the involved parties refuses to cooperate in resolving the issue.

- You mediate conflict resolution between two employees, believe that the problem has been solved, and later discover that one (or both) of the involved parties failed to do what was agreed upon.

A Few Tips on How to do it:

➤ Meet with each uncooperative employee individually. Describe the problem in terms of *the specific behavior you expect* from him or her vs. *what he or she has actually done* – or NOT done. Review any history of the problem (e.g., if you have talked about it before) and the impact it is having on your work group … and on YOU.

➤ Ask for an explanation: *What's happening … What's going on here?* Listen to what he or she has to say. Make sure there are no mitigating circumstances that prevented him or her from meeting your expectations. If you hear something that indicates the person may not be at fault, suspend the meeting until you've had time to investigate.

➤ Tell the person what he or she must do. Clarify, in specific behavioral terms, exactly what actions you expect him or her to take in order to help resolve the conflict. And review the consequences he or she will face if your expectations aren't met.

➤ Monitor the situation and follow up to ensure compliance with your mandate. If your expectations are met, acknowledge and thank the involved parties. If your expectations aren't met, initiate the consequences you identified.

Finale and Farewell

Closing Thoughts

With few exceptions, none of us consciously chooses to have conflict in our lives. It just seems to happen. But ...

we DO choose how we'll *respond* to conflict when we find it staring us in the face.

And when the issues we're facing affect our ability to perform at work, it's critically important that we choose wisely.

The old saying *We're all in this together* is especially true when it comes to business organizations. We really *are* interdependent. We need each other ... we rely on each other. We must work together to attain the success each of us wants and needs. Clearly, anything that gets in the way of that success is an enemy to all – one that must be dealt with and eliminated. The stakes are too high to do anything less.

So, the next time you find yourself involved in a workplace conflict, don't run from it or let it fester until you eventually explode. Instead, choose to apply the tools and strategies this book has provided. Use what you've learned to make your working time less stressful and more fulfilling.

To be sure, interpersonal conflicts are workplace realities. But *unresolved* conflicts don't have to be.

The key is knowing what to do when conflict happens ... and doing it!

The greatest ability
in business is
to get along with others
and influence their actions.
A chip on the shoulder
is too heavy
a piece of baggage
to carry through life.

~ John A. Hannah

The Authors

Eric Harvey is a renowned author, consultant, speaker, and president of The WALK THE TALK® Company. His 30-plus years of professional experience are reflected in 26 highly acclaimed books, including the best-selling *WALK THE TALK And Get The Results You Want*, *The Leadership Secrets of Santa Claus*®, *Ethics4Everyone*, and *Leadership Courage*.

Steve Ventura is a recognized and respected author, educator, book producer, and award-winning training program designer. His work reflects over thirty years of human resource development experience – both as a practitioner and a business consultant. His prior books include *Start Right...Stay Right*, *Walk Awhile in My Shoes*, *Five Star Teamwork*, and *Lead Right*.

The Publisher

For over 30 years, WalkTheTalk.com has been dedicated to one simple goal... one single mission: ***To provide you and your organization with high-impact resources for your personal and professional success.***
Walk The Talk resources are designed to:

- Develop your skills and confidence
- Inspire your team
- Create customer enthusiasm
- Build leadership skills
- Stretch your mind
- Handle tough "people problems"
- Develop a culture of respect and responsibility
- And, most importantly, help you achieve your personal and professional goals.

Contact the Walk The Talk team at
1.888.822.9255
or visit us at
www.walkthetalk.com

Introducing:

What To Do When CONFLICT HAPPENS
Group Training Package!

This video-based program gives people solid skills for resolving workplace conflict. By seeing the C.A.L.M. Model in action, and practicing the techniques in a group setting, participants gain the confidence to address day-to-day conflicts as they arise.

Each step in the process is explored in detail:

Clarify the Issue.
Address the Problem.
Listen to the Other Side.
Manage Your Way to Resolution.

Training Program Includes:

- Training DVD
- Leader's Guide
- PowerPoint Presentation on CD-ROM
- 10 Participant Workbooks
- 10 copies of the *What To Do When CONFLICT HAPPENS* Handbook

Complete Program: $995

For more information and to see a FREE Preview, visit
www.walkthetalk.com

What To Do When CONFLICT HAPPENS

1-99 Copies	**$10.95**
100-499 Copies	**$9.95**
500+ Copies	**Please Call**

Other recommended resources from WalkTheTalk.com

Positive Discipline – Practical time-tested techniques for resolving performance problems ... while strengthening employee commitment in the process. Within these pages, your people will find the tools they need in order to get the results you want. $10.95

The Manager's Coaching Handbook – The Manager's Coaching Handbook provides managers, supervisors, and team leaders with simple, easy-to-follow guidelines for positively affecting employee performance. $10.95

Better yet, consider the Workplace Problem Solving Kit!

3 best-selling Walk The Talk books packed with ideas and strategies to Resolve Tough Performance Problems Quickly...and Permanently!
This kit contains the following Walk The Talk books:
Positive Discipline
What To Do When CONFLICT HAPPENS
The Manager's Coaching Handbook

This kit is jam-packed with tips and strategies to help you:
Identify a Performance Problem
Conduct Performance Improvement Sessions
Follow Up On Performance Improvement Sessions
Set the Pace For Future Success   ONLY $29.95!

ORDER FORM

Have questions? Need assistance? Call 1.888.822.9255

☑ **Please send me additional copies of What To Do When CONFLICT HAPPENS**

1-99 copies: $10.95 ea.   100-499 copies: $9.95 ea.   500+ copies: *call 1.888.822.9255*

What To Do When CONFLICT HAPPENS _____ copies X $_____ = $_____

Additional Resources

What To Do When CONFLICT HAPPENS Group Training Package	_____ pkgs.	X $ 995.00 =	$_____
Positive Discipline	_____ copies	X $ 10.95 =	$_____
The Manager's Coaching Handbook	_____ copies	X $ 10.95 =	$_____
Workplace Problem Solving Kit	_____ copies	X $ 29.95 =	$_____

Product Total $_____
* Shipping & Handling $_____
Subtotal $_____

(Sales Tax Collected on TX Customers Only)

Sales Tax:
TX Sales Tax – 8.25% $_____
TOTAL (U.S. Dollars Only) $_____

---

*Shipping and Handling Charges
For actual shipping rates, please visit *WalkTheTalk.com*

Name_____ Title _____

Organization _____

Shipping Address _____
No P. O. Boxes

City_____ State_____ Zip _____

Phone _____ Fax _____

E-Mail _____

Charge Your Order: ❏ MasterCard   ❏ Visa   ❏ American Express

Credit Card Number_____ Exp. _____

❏ Check Enclosed (Payable to: The WALK THE TALK Company)

❏ Please Invoice (Orders over $250 ONLY)   P. O. # (required) _____

Prices effective January, 2010 are subject to change.

PHONE
1.888.822.9255
or 972.899.8300
M-F, 8:30 – 5:00 Central

ONLINE
www.walkthetalk.com

FAX
972.899.9291

MAIL
WALK THE TALK CO.
1100 Parker Square, Suite 250
Flower Mound, TX 75028